3 JAZZ SUITES
FOR PIANO

By Glenda Austin

ISBN 978-1-5400-7252-8

WILLIS MUSIC®

EXCLUSIVELY DISTRIBUTED BY

HAL•LEONARD®

Visit Hal Leonard Online at
www.halleonard.com

World headquarters, contact:
Hal Leonard
7777 West Bluemound Road
Milwaukee, WI 53213
Email: info@halleonard.com

In Europe, contact:
Hal Leonard Europe Limited
1 Red Place
London, W1K 6PL
Email: info@halleonardeurope.com

In Australia, contact:
Hal Leonard Australia Pty. Ltd.
4 Lentara Court
Cheltenham, Victoria, 3192 Australia
Email: info@halleonard.com.au

NOTES FROM THE COMPOSER

Jazz Suite No. 1 in F Major
(published 1985)

MID-INTERMEDIATE

My first jazz suite came together as a result of three individual pieces. Early in my composing days, I wrote several short pieces and wondered what to do with them. William Gillock, a close friend, suggested selecting a few that might go together to form a "suite." Well, this was it! The 2nd movement was originally in the key of A Minor and was transposed to F Minor when paired with the other two pieces. Fun fact: I often write the 2nd movement first (not sure why) and then build around it.

Jazz Suite No. 2 in B-flat Major
(published 2001)

MID TO LATER INTERMEDIATE

The second jazz suite was written to commemorate the retirement of my much-loved college piano professor, Raymond Herbert, and was inspired by several of my favorite pieces. The 1st movement has a hint of George Gershwin's second piano prelude in C-sharp Minor. I'm often asked if I am aware of that—yes, I am! And I'm very glad you noticed! The 2nd movement, a light jazz waltz, was influenced by Claude Bolling's *Suite for Flute and Jazz Piano* (1973). If you don't know it, please take a few minutes to listen—it's a fantastic piece of music! And finally, the 3rd movement (and the most difficult) has a hint of a very popular, late 1950s TV show about an American private eye. We were always glued to the TV, and I loved the theme song. Back then, I never dreamed any inspiration would come from this show, but it sure did! (Figured it out, yet? Answer is at the bottom of the page.)*

Jazz Suite No. 3 in F Major
(published 2020)

EARLY TO MID-INTERMEDIATE

Commissioned by the Music Teachers National Association and originally written as a chamber trio (piano, clarinet, and percussion), my third jazz suite was set to premiere at the 2020 National Conference in Chicago. Because of the Covid pandemic, the convention was cancelled, which was historically unprecedented. The piece was officially premiered at the 2021 conference, held virtually.

It was challenging and rewarding to transcribe it as a piano solo. The 2nd movement was written first and began with a rhythmic idea to incorporate triplets against duplets. Though it may initially present a challenge to balance the rhythms, the result should be a sumptuous, sophisticated sound. The 3rd movement has much thinner texture and is heavy on syncopation, speed, and show. There are cued notes to play as octaves for the very brave! The 1st movement was inspired from my days of playing in a ragtime band.

What an interesting few months it has been, adapting Suite No. 3 for piano solo as well as revising and fine-tuning the first two suites. These are the definitive versions.

Glenda Austin

March 2020 *(revised October 2023)*

*Peter Gunn.

CONTENTS

To David

Jazz Suite No. 1

Glenda Austin

I. PRELUDE. Moderato ♩ = 112–120

II. INTERLUDE. Andante cantabile con rubato ♩ = 76–88 ♪♪ = ♪♪

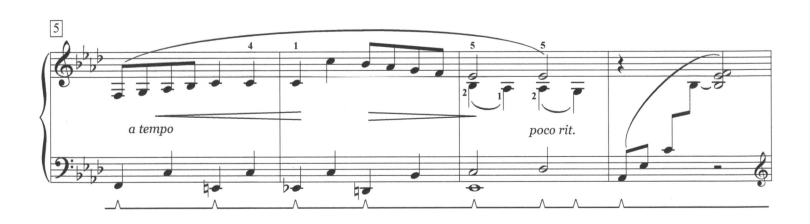

8

III. FINALE. Allegro con brio ♩ = 88–112 (hang on!)

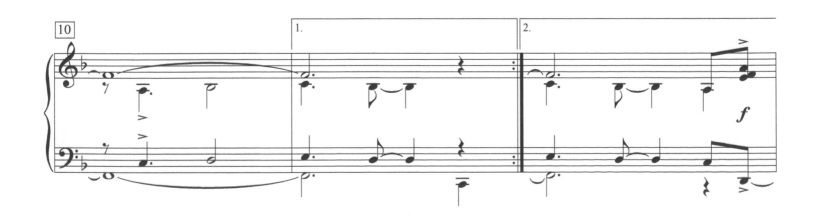

To commemorate the retirement of
Professor Raymond Herbert, University of Missouri, 2001

Jazz Suite No. 2

Glenda Austin

I. Andante con moto ed un poco rubato

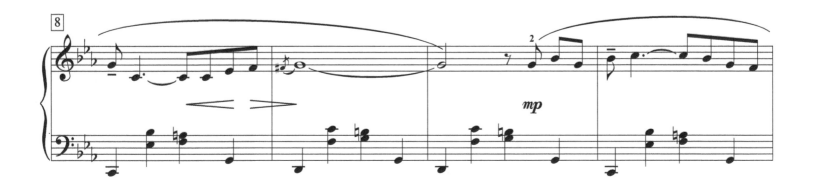

* May be swung if desired.

III. Presto e deciso ♩ = 144–176

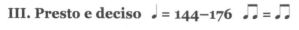

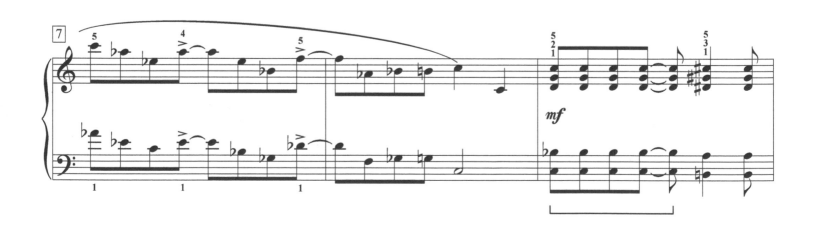

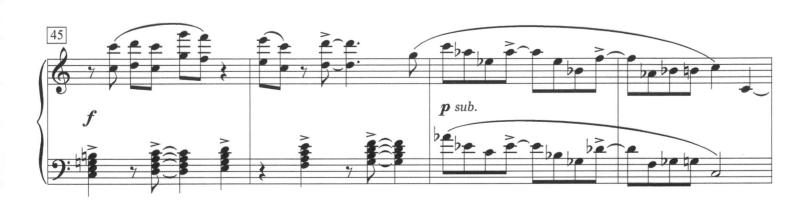

Jazz Suite No. 3

This piece was commissioned for MTNA 2020 and
was originally written for clarinet, cajón, and piano.

Glenda Austin

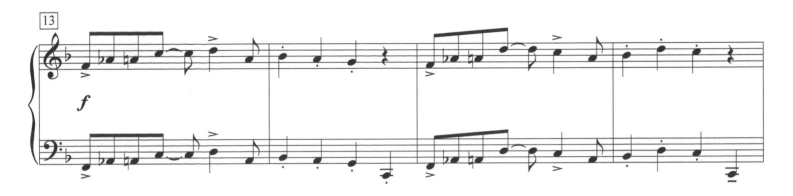

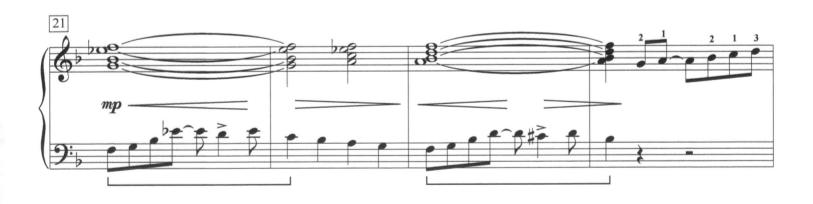

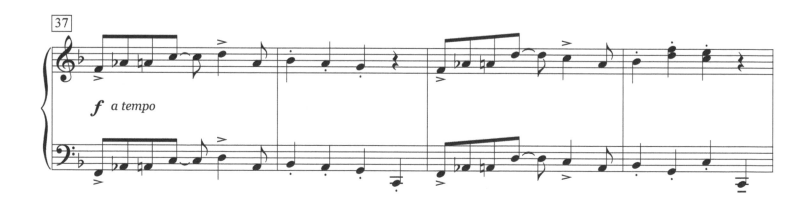

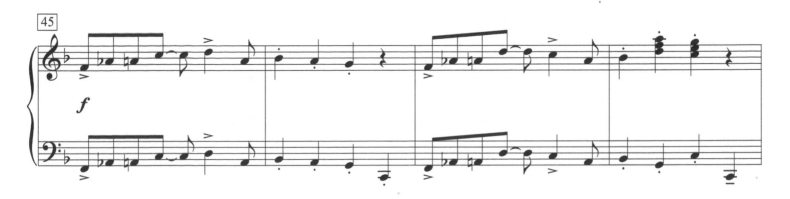

II. Freely flowing, with flexibility ♩ = 76–88

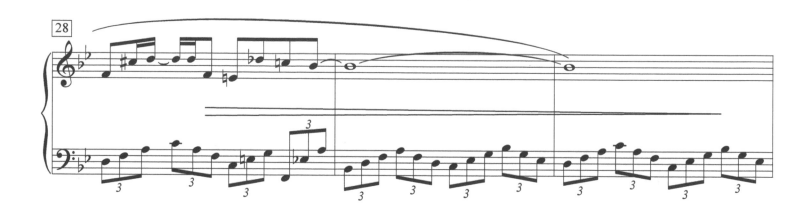

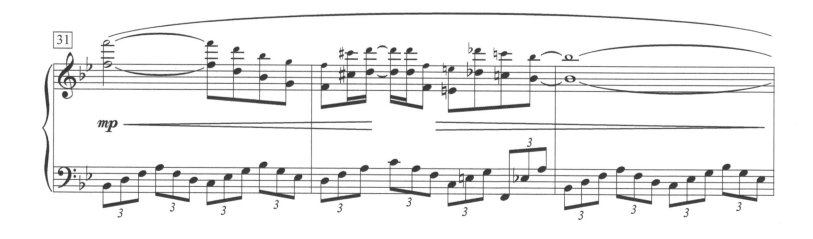

III. Intriguing and mysterious ♩ = 112–120 ♫ = ♫

Pedal lightly throughout

* **Optional:** R.H. glissando to the highest F of the piano.